CANOEING
A BEGINNER'S GUIDE TO THE KAYAK

CANOEING
A BEGINNER'S GUIDE TO THE KAYAK

Nigel Foster
Photographs by Julia Claxton

Fernhurst Books

First published 1990 by Fernhurst Books,
31 Church Road, Hove, East Sussex

British Library Cataloguing in Publication Data

Foster, Nigel
   Canoeing: A Beginner's Guide to the Kayak
   1. Canoeing
   I. Title
   797.1'22
   ISBN 0 906754 50 X

Printed and bound in Great Britain

Acknowledgements

The author would like to thank Martyn Hedges of Bushsport, David Train of Elliott Trading Ltd, Alistair Wilson of Lendal Products Ltd, Jane and Graham Goldsmith of Perception Kayaks UK, Sola Wetsuits and Chris Hawkesworth of Wildwater for their assistance with equipment.

   Thanks are also due to Geoff Good of the British Canoe Union for his helpful comments on the manuscript, and Bob Bond of Plas Menai for his assistance with the project.

   The photographs on pages 8, 42, 44, 47, 49, 60 and on the cover were supplied by Tickle Design Group. The book design is by Nick Cannan, and the cover design by Joyce Chester.

Composition by Central Southern Typesetters, Hove
Printed by Ebenezer Baylis & Son Ltd, Worcester

Contents

1   What you will need   6

2   Preparing to go afloat   9

3   Your first paddle   14

4   Forward paddling, reversing and stopping   17

5   Basic turning   20

6   Moving sideways   22

7   Steering and turning on the move   25

8   Rescue   28

9   Support, recovery and sculling strokes   35

10 The bow rudder turn and hanging draw   44

11 The Eskimo roll   48

12 Equipment   55

13 Safety   64

1 What you will need _____

This chapter outlines the basic gear you will need for your first time afloat (for more detail, and for a greater range of available equipment, see Chapter 12).

The kayak

The *kayak*, often called a 'canoe' in Britain, is a craft that you sit in, facing forwards, and propel with a double-bladed paddle. The *canoe* ('Canadian canoe' in Britain) is a craft in which you kneel down to paddle with a single-bladed paddle. This book concerns itself with the kayak.

Kayaks come in many different shapes, depending on what they are designed to do, but they should all have a hull and deck, a cockpit with a seat, buoyancy, a footrest and 'end grabs'.

The hull is the underside of the kayak, and the deck is the covering over the top. The cockpit is the opening in which the seat is positioned. There must be some form of fixed buoyancy inside the kayak, sufficient to float the kayak and also support a swimmer even when the kayak is filled with water. The buoyancy must be distributed in both ends of the kayak so that it floats level when

Above *A white-water 'fun' kayak (**left**), the Dancer, and (**right**) a placid-water touring kayak, the Poly Pippin.*

Below *Buoyancy must be fixed in both ends. Here, central pillars of polyethylene foam are supplemented by the use of air bags.*

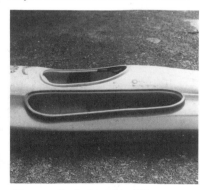

Above *Cockpit styles. The touring kayak (foreground) has a large, 'open' cockpit, while the white-water kayak behind has a smaller, 'closed' cockpit.*

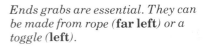

*Ends grabs are essential. They can be made from rope (**far left**) or a toggle (**left**).*

full of water. Buoyancy most commonly takes the form of shaped blocks of polyethylene or polystyrene foam which are fixed between the hull and the deck, providing rigidity and strength, or air bags, which may also be used as additional buoyancy to fill the spaces on either side of foam blocks.

A footrest is essential for efficient paddling technique. The footrest may take the form of a fixed pedal for each foot, adjustable along a track; a bar across the inside of the kayak, fastened to a flange on either side; or an adjustable bulkhead or 'full-plate' footrest.

At each end of the kayak there should be an 'end grab'. This may be of rope or tape, and usually features a toggle. End grabs should be easy to find when the kayak is overturned, and it should not be possible for your fingers to become trapped, as they might be by a simple rope loop, if the kayak rolled over in the water.

In addition, you may have deck-lines running along or across the deck. These are not essential, but are very useful as handholds during rescues on the water, and when lifting and handling the kayak. For safety, deck-lines must not be able to foul the cockpit area, and must be kept taut so that they cannot entangle you.

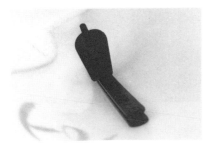

*Footrests. The pedal footrest (**above**) can be adjusted along a track.*

The full-plate footrest – probably the most comfortable.

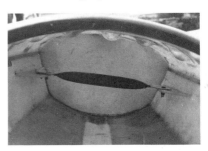

Bar footrest with fail-safe device to prevent feet jamming.

The paddle

The paddle consists of a shaft (sometimes known as the loom), with a paddle blade at each end. The shaft should be oval in section at least towards one end, to help you position your hands correctly. The blades are normally set at 80 to 90 degrees to one another, and are curved. The concave surface of the blade is called the *drive face* or *power face*, and the convex surface is called the *back* of the blade.

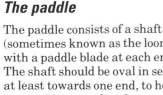

blade

shaft or loom

back of blade

drive or
power face

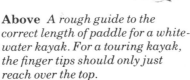

Above *A rough guide to the correct length of paddle for a white-water kayak. For a touring kayak, the finger tips should only just reach over the top.*

The kayak paddle has two blades at nearly right angles to each other.

Buoyancy aid or personal flotation device

Wearing a buoyancy aid is essential for safety. The International Canoe Federation recommends that there should be a minimum of 6 kilograms (13 lb) of inherent buoyancy. In Britain the most common design is a waistcoat-shaped jacket, with panels of buoyant foam in the front and back, and often also in the sides. The garment is either pulled on over the head, or fastened down the front, and should be fastened around the waist to prevent the jacket riding up your body when you are in the water. Whatever buoyancy aid you choose, it should be a good fit – not too loose nor too tight – and should be fitted according to the manufacturer's instructions.

The foam used in many buoyancy aids will deteriorate with age, gradually losing buoyancy. Simple care will maximize its useful life. Sitting on the buoyancy aid compresses the buoyancy, which is bad news. I always rinse my buoyancy aid in fresh water and hang it to dry after each use. It is best stored hanging up indoors.

Clothing

You will need some clothing suitable to the conditions and the weather. You will be colder on the water than on dry land, especially if you get wet, but reflected sunshine from the water may cause your skin to burn more easily. Whatever clothing you choose to wear, it should keep you warm even when wet, should not prevent you from swimming, and should resist the wind. Wool is excellent when wet for retaining heat, particularly when worn under a windproof jacket. Together with tracksuit trousers and running shoes, this would make a good combination for a first time afloat. There is a wide choice of specialist canoeing clothing available nowadays, including wet suits and dry suits. This is described at the end of the book.

White-water slalom competition, Seo 'd'Ugell, Spain (photo: Tickle Design Group).

There are a few preparations to make before you venture on to the water.

Getting in to your kayak

Check that your kayak is properly equipped as described in Chapter 1. Next, you will need to adjust the footrest to fit your leg length. Place the kayak on a soft surface such as grass, and sit in it. Adjust the footrest until your feet rest lightly on it. You should be able to brace both feet firmly against the footrest while pressing your knees against the inside of the kayak to either side of the cockpit, but you should also be able to relax and straighten your legs, bringing your knees together. This adjustment is worth getting right. If the footrest is too close, your legs will soon become uncomfortable, and may grow numb. If the footrest is too distant, you will not have full control of your kayak.

Practising 'trunk rotation'

With your footrest in position, sit upright in the kayak with your feet resting lightly on the footrest. Now press gently against the footrest with your right foot, straightening your right leg and twisting your upper body to the right; your left knee should be allowed to bend to help this movement. Your right shoulder should now be above the back of your cockpit while your left shoulder is above the front. Now twist in a similar manner towards the left, pressing this time with your left foot.

This twisting of your body ('trunk rotation') is a major source of power when you are paddling forwards, and differing degrees of rotation are needed to position yourself correctly for many other strokes.

Above *Adjusting your footrest (white-water kayak). You should be able to relax your legs (top picture) or brace firmly (lower picture).*

Above *With the footrest correctly adjusted in a placid-water touring kayak, the knees will protrude from the cockpit for normal paddling.*

Practising trunk rotation.

1

2

3

4

5

6

Practise getting in to your kayak on dry land. Lay the paddle within easy reach. With one hand on the bank and the other at the centre of the rear deck, place one foot in the cockpit (1, 2). Sit on the back deck and bring your other foot into the cockpit (3). Slide your feet down *inside the kayak (4). Ease yourself into your seat, still holding the bank with one hand (5). Finally, take up your paddle (6).*

Getting out of your kayak

Place both hands behind you on the back (stern) deck, one to each side behind the cockpit. Relax your legs and push with your hands to ease yourself on to the back deck. This is how to escape from your kayak if you overturn on the water, but in that event you will not have to lift yourself against the pull of gravity.

Now try to lift yourself on to the back deck using only one hand. This is useful practice for getting out on to land, when you will probably need your other hand to hold on to the shore. Place your hand on the centre line of the kayak to stop it tipping.

Your paddles

Stand with your paddle held vertically in front of you, with the drive face of the lower blade towards your toes. The drive face of the upper blade will be facing left if your paddle is designed for control with the left hand, or right if the paddle is for right-hand control. The illustrations in this book show paddlers using right-hand control paddles; to see the hand positions for a left-hand control paddle, simply look at the photographs in a mirror.

Grasp your paddle with your hands spaced just a little wider than the width of your kayak.

Left *Left or right hand control? Stand with the drive face of the lower blade towards your toes. If the upper blade curves towards your right, the paddle is for right-hand control.*
Below *Getting out. Place your paddle gently on shore; hold the bank with one hand, and the centre of your rear deck with the other. Ease yourself out to sit on the rear deck. Now you can bring your feet back to the seat and step out, still holding the kayak.*

Two ways of gauging the correct hand spacing. Left, just a little wider than the width of your kayak. Right, a little wider than your shoulders.

Your hands should be on top of the shaft, with your thumbs underneath. The distance between your hand and the paddle blade should be the same on each side. Hold the paddles at arm's length horizontally in front of you, at shoulder height, with the drive face of the blade on your control side facing you. If your paddle shaft is oval only towards one end, hold this end in your control hand.

Now relax your non-control hand, allowing the paddle shaft to rotate freely in that hand. Grip with your control hand and bend it upwards from the wrist so that the palm faces ahead; this rotates the paddle through about 90 degrees, until the drive face of the non-control blade now faces you. Now reverse the movement, bringing the palm of your control hand downwards again until the drive face of your control blade faces you once more. This action, similar to operating the throttle of a motorcycle, is the movement you make to adjust the angle of the

paddle in the water. Your non-control hand does not move, allowing the paddle shaft to rotate freely; this gives you full control of both blades with your control hand.

Below *A dry run through the paddling action. The 'throttle' action can be seen in frames 3, 4 and 6.*

Above *The 'throttle' action used to control your paddles. Left, hold your paddle at arm's length, with the right-hand blade on edge (in position for a forward stroke). Right, rotate your paddle through 90° by lifting the palm of your control hand to face ahead. The left blade is now ready for a forward stroke.*

1

2

3

Where should I paddle?

Find a stretch of fairly calm, non-moving water for your first paddle, ideally with low or gently shelving banks. This might be a pond, lake or canal. Make sure you have the permission of the landowner to use the water. Ideally, for your first time afloat, go with an experienced paddler. Otherwise, use common sense and have a companion on the shore who is prepared and able to help you in case of difficulties. Do not paddle alone. Have a look at Chapter 13 for some other safety recommendations.

Right *Carrying your kayak.* **Top row** *Lift the kayak by the front of the cockpit and place your shoulder in the cockpit, with the stern still resting on the ground.* **Bottom row** *Lean forwards slightly to balance the kayak on your shoulder. A well-practised flick of the foot will bring your paddle into your hand.*

4

5

6

3 Your first paddle

How do I get afloat?

To prevent damage to the kayak,
make sure it is afloat before you
get in. Put your paddles on the
shore within easy reach of your
kayak. Sit down in your kayak,
keeping your weight as low as
possible while you get in to
maintain your balance. Brace your
feet lightly against the footrest
and your knees against the inside
of the kayak, pick up your paddles,
and away you go!

How do I control my kayak?

The nearer to your kayak you
make your paddle strokes, the
straighter you will run. Remember
to rotate your body to gain the
maximum reach towards the front
(bow) of your kayak, pulling back
the paddle at the same time as you
pull back your shoulder, rotating
your body in the other direction.
Your other arm should push
forwards at shoulder height to
keep the paddle away from your
chest.

   The further out from the kayak
you sweep your paddle, the more
easily it will turn. You can sweep
from the front to the back or vice
versa. Try to lead the paddle in a
semicircular path when you want
to turn.

How do I get out?

Paddle to the shore and hold on
firmly to the bank with one hand.
Place your paddles gently on dry
land – do not throw them, as they
are easily damaged. Gently climb
out in the same way you have
practised on dry land. Don't worry
if you are a little awkward at first,
you will soon become more nimble!

Above *Getting afloat. Make sure the kayak is floating. Place your paddle
within easy reach. Keep your weight low while you get in.*

Above *Make your paddle strokes near to the kayak to keep straight.
Forward paddling is explained in more detail in the next chapter.*

*Landing. Place your paddle gently on the shore, then climb out as you
have practised on dry land.*

What happens if I overturn?

It is a good idea to make your first capsize a deliberate and controlled one, with a companion standing by if only for moral support.

Check the depth of the water with your paddle: just over a metre (about 4 ft) should be plenty, and will allow you to stand up following your exit.

Place your hands behind you, one hand retaining the paddle, and lean to one side until you overbalance. Holding your breath, relax your legs and gently ease the kayak away from you with both hands, as if you were shedding a pair of trousers.

Hold your paddles with one hand, while keeping contact with your kayak with the other, and surface beside your upturned craft.

Your buoyancy aid will keep you afloat, so relax. Leave the kayak upside down, and disturb it as little as possible. It will hold air inside in this position, which will prevent further water from entering. Without losing contact with the kayak, take hold of the end grab and swim it to the shore, holding your paddles in your other hand.

Above *Open cockpits are designed to allow you to fall out as you capsize. Leave your kayak upside down while you swim it to the shore. Keep hold of both your kayak and your paddle.*

Capsize procedure for a closed cockpit kayak. Once upside down, use both hands to ease yourself out. Again, never let go of kayak or paddle.

How do I empty the water out?

Solo, lift one end of the kayak on to the shore until it is a few centimetres (inches) above the water level. Then lift the other end, holding it on either side about half a metre (2 ft) from the end to prevent it from rolling upright. Most of the water will drain out through the cockpit. Now place this end on the shore too, and lift the first end. Repeat the procedure until your kayak is empty, then roll the kayak upright.

If you have assistance, each person takes an end, and you lift each end in turn to drain out the water. It is also possible to empty a kayak and re-enter while in deep water, with the aid of another kayaker. This is called a *deep-water rescue*, and is described in Chapter 8.

Emptying a kayak. **Right** *Lift one end on to the shore. All the water will drain from that end. Then raise the lower end to complete the emptying. It's quicker with someone to help you (***below***).*

— 4 *Forward paddling, reversing and stopping*

Now you have been afloat and have some idea of how to control a kayak in the water, you can begin to refine the individual strokes. Most of your paddling will be forwards, so we shall look at forward paddling technique first. For convenience I refer to the arm nearest the water (the right arm if the right blade is in the water) as the 'bottom' arm, and the other as the 'top' arm.

Forward paddling

The starting position for the stroke

1 Stretch your bottom arm forward, bringing your shoulder forward by rotating the body to increase your reach.

2 The top arm is bent, shoulder back; the palm of the hand faces forwards with the fingers open, ready to push forwards.
3 Straighten the leg on the same side as your bottom arm, ready to push against the footrest.
4 Relax the leg on the other side, with the knee ready to rise as the leg on the stroke side straightens.

The stroke itself

Place the paddle blade in the water close beside the kayak, and pull the kayak past it using the power from your trunk rotation, begun by pressing against the footrest on the same side as your paddle. Pull with your bottom arm, at the same time pushing your top arm forwards with fingers extended. It

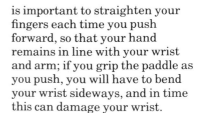

is important to straighten your fingers each time you push forward, so that your hand remains in line with your wrist and arm; if you grip the paddle as you push, you will have to bend your wrist sideways, and in time this can damage your wrist.

As your top shoulder reaches its forward position with the trunk fully rotated, the blade will be by your side. Slip the blade sideways out of the water and place the other blade in the water for the next stroke.

Once you have mastered the movement step by step, concentrate on making your forward paddling a smooth, continuous action rather than a series of separate movements.

Forward paddling, viewed from the front.

Stretch your bottom arm forwards.

Push your top arm forward with straight fingers.

Slip the blade sideways out of the water and repeat the stroke on the other side.

Forward paddling. Bring your shoulder forwards to increase your reach. Place the blade in the water, with the fingers of the top hand extended.

Pull the kayak past the blade using the power from your trunk rotation. Slip the blade sideways out of the water.

Place the other blade in the water for the next stroke.

Keeping straight

If your kayak starts to run off course, say to the left, then place your paddle in the water on the left, well out from the side of your kayak behind the cockpit, and sweep it powerfully in to the stern as far back as you can easily reach.

Right *If you run off course, put your paddle in the water to that side and pull the blade in to the stern* (**far right**).

Stopping

If you are moving forwards, reverse to stop, and if you are moving backwards, paddle forwards to stop. With practice you will only need two to four rapid but positive paddle strokes to stop completely, even if you are travelling fast. Practise until you can stop quickly without turning at all, and without having to concentrate on what you are doing.

Right *Stopping. Four positive reverse strokes should be enough.*

Reversing

When reversing, use the back of your paddle blade so that you do not alter the position of your control hand on the shaft.

The starting position for the stroke
1 Rotate your body so that the blade is ready to enter the water close to the kayak, just behind you.
2 Your bottom arm should be slightly bent, ready to push the blade down and forwards.
3 Bring your top hand across to the same side of the kayak as your bottom hand, so that the paddle shaft is held almost parallel to the kayak.
4 To prevent yourself sliding back in your seat, brace against the kayak with the knee or thigh on the side that you are making your paddle stroke.
5 Turn your head to see where you are going.

The stroke itself
1 Push down and forwards with your bottom arm and rotate your body. Keep the blade close to your kayak.
2 Keeping your top arm fairly straight in order to keep the paddle away from your body, guide the top blade across the front deck as your body rotates.
3 Maximum paddling efficiency is achieved when the paddle blade is upright in the water, which will be from a position roughly level with

your hip to a point close to your knee. When the blade reaches your knee, lift it out sideways from the water, placing the other blade in the starting position for the next stroke.

Keeping straight
You will not have perfect rear vision, so keep a frequent lookout over your shoulder while you paddle backwards. Choosing a target to paddle towards will help you get into the habit, and will

also develop your directional control.

If your kayak runs off course to one side, bring it back on course by making a wider sweep on that side with the back of your paddle blade. Push the blade out from the stern and bring it in to finish powerfully as far forward as you can reach. This should certainly be beyond your feet. Do not lift the blade out of the water until it has almost touched the side of the kayak.

Reversing: keep paddle blades close to the kayak for a straight course. Use the back of the blade. Remember to look behind you!

5 Basic turning

The basic turn uses a stroke called the *sweep stroke*. It is mainly a turn to be used when you are stationary and want to turn around, but like most basic strokes, it may be modified for use on the move. Turning on the move is described in Chapter 7.

The forward sweep

1 Reach forward as far as possible with one blade, rotating your body. The edge of the blade should be in the water, rather than its end, with the drive face away from the kayak.

2 Pull the blade out from the bow steadily in a wide semicircle towards the back of the kayak. The kayak will turn. Watch the blade as you pull it in to the stern, then lift it out smartly as it reaches the kayak.

3 Repeat the stroke, but at the same time push the paddle across the kayak with the top arm so that the shaft is parallel to the kayak at the end of the stroke.

4 Now, to get a greater reach, lean forwards for the start of each stroke, and back at the end of each stroke.

5 To give you more power and control, push gently with the foot on the same side as your paddle stroke.

This stroke is most efficient when the paddle is stationary in the water and the kayak moves. If you sweep too vigorously, the paddle will move through the water and you will lose power.

Right *The forward sweep.*

The reverse sweep

1 Reach back as far as you can with the paddle held in its normal grip. Place the paddle in the water by the stern of your kayak, with the blade on edge and the drive face towards the kayak.

2 Your top hand should reach across the kayak so that the paddle shaft is parallel to the kayak for the start of the stroke.

3 Push the blade steadily out from the stern in a wide semicircle, bringing it in powerfully to the bow.

4 Your top hand should guide the paddle shaft across the kayak, keeping the paddle away from your chest.

5 Lean back at the start of the stroke, and forwards at the end, to give you maximum reach.

If you sweep alternately forwards on one side and reverse on the other, your kayak will spin around on the spot. If you use repeated sweeps on one side only, your kayak will move across the water in a wider circle.

Left *The reverse sweep.*

6 Moving sideways

The two most important ways of moving your kayak sideways are the *draw stroke* and the *sculling draw*. The sculling draw is described in Chapter 9. In the draw stroke, described below, you place your paddle out to one side of you, vertically in the water with the drive face towards you, and pull your kayak towards it.

The draw stroke

The starting position for the stroke

Once you have learnt this stroke you will use exactly the same hand grip and spacing on the paddles as for forward paddling. However, the stroke is easier to learn with the hands in a 'practice' position.

Move your hands down the paddle shaft until your bottom hand is grasping the neck of the blade itself, and the top hand is just a little more than the width of the kayak away from it. The hand grip is otherwise exactly the same

as for normal paddling.
1 Twist your body to face your intended direction of travel.
2 Reach out to the side and plant your whole paddle blade in the water. Your hand should now be just touching the water.
3 Extend your top arm to bring the shaft of the paddle as upright as possible. You are now in the starting position for the stroke.

The stroke itself

1 Pull gently with your bottom arm and push away with your top arm.
2 When the blade reaches the side of your kayak, twist the blade so that the edge of the blade is towards you and the drive face is towards the stern of the kayak.
3 Slice the blade cleanly away from you through the water and turn it again at arm's length into the starting position once more.
4 Repeat the sequence until it becomes fluent.

Above *The paddle held in the 'practice' position.* **Below** *The draw stroke viewed from the side.* **Opposite** *The complete draw stroke.*

1

2

3

4

5

6

7

8

9

How do I control my sideways direction?

The kayak will often wander off in a circle instead of moving sideways in a straight line. This can easily be corrected by drawing the paddle towards a point a little further forward or to a point a little further back than usual.

Use the same starting position as before, which should be about level with your body. Angle the blade towards the front of the cockpit and draw it steadily towards the front of the cockpit with the blade at that angle. The front of your kayak should move more quickly than the stern, turning you. When the blade reaches the kayak, twist the blade edge-on to the starting point and slice it cleanly away. If you repeat the stroke you will eventually turn a full circle, facing towards the outside of the circle.

To turn in the other direction, go back to the starting position once more. Angle the blade towards the back of the cockpit, and draw it steadily to the back of the cockpit before turning it edge-on towards

the starting point. The drive face should be towards the stern. Slice the blade back out and repeat the stroke. You will now be drawing the stern faster than the bow, and should gradually turn a full circle, facing into the centre of the circle.

You should now be able to steer your kayak along a straight path, turning it back on course should it stray.

The draw stroke with the correct hand position

Hold your paddle in the normal forward paddling position. When you reach out into the starting position for the draw stroke, immerse the blade to the point where your bottom hand is just touching the water. The stroke is performed then exactly as practised, but you will find it much more powerful. Because of this, be ready to twist the blade edge-on to the kayak as soon as your bottom hand reaches the kayak, or you may easily be overturned.

Practise the draw stroke by setting yourself a target to aim towards. You should become

controlled and fluent in both directions: to the left and to the right.

A white-water variation

In white-water kayaking, for example when positioning the kayak to negotiate a rapid, only one or two draw strokes may be needed, and you will need to look forwards rather than to the side. Try using the following technique.

Position your top hand close to your forehead and do not rotate your trunk. The paddle blade will enter the water at an angle of about 45 degrees. As you draw your bottom hand towards the kayak, push your top hand across to bring the paddle as upright as possible. You will now be looking forwards beneath your arm rather than above it, and your blade will be much closer to the surface than in the basic draw stroke.

This variation is useful for white-water kayaking, especially in shallow water, so practise it instead of the basic stroke if you are planning take up this branch of the sport.

Above *Using the same starting position, but drawing the paddle towards the front of the cockpit, causes the bow to move faster than the stern.*

Below *Rafting up.*

Rafting up

'Rafting up' is the parking of one kayak alongside another, or others, to form a stable platform. It can be used to provide stability while afloat for tasks such as climbing out of your seat to extract a flask of coffee from the back of your kayak, or emptying out gravel from your shoes.

Once your kayaks are safely together, place your paddles across

your laps, close beneath your buoyancy aids, and hold on to the kayaks beside you towards the front end of the cockpit. This will prevent your paddles from rolling away, and will ensure that the raft does not disintegrate.

Rafting up is an excellent way of practising your manoeuvring skills, demanding a combination of forward and backward, turning and draw strokes. In addition, your

target will probably be moving or rotating as you attempt to dock. For maximum benefit of your practice, alternate between approaching from the left, and approaching from the right.

In this chapter we look at the *stern rudder* as a way to steer your kayak on a straight course, and the *low brace turn* as a method of turning on the move.

The stern rudder

Paddling at an angle downwind can be quite difficult. The effect of wind and waves will cause most kayaks to broach, turning broadside or into the wind. If the paddle blade is held still in the water near the stern, it will act as a rudder to counter this turning effect. The stern rudder will only work if you are moving through the water.

1 Start with the paddle held in the same position as for the start of a reverse sweep stroke (the paddle shaft parallel alongside the kayak, with the blade on edge in the water well behind you). This is the 'neutral' position, which should have no noticeable turning effect on the kayak.

2 Tilting the blade so that the upper edge is further from the kayak than the lower edge will make the kayak turn towards the paddle. You will need to push down on the paddle a little to prevent the paddle from moving.

3 Tilting the blade so that the upper edge is closer to the kayak than the lower edge will make the kayak turn away from the paddle. You will need to pull down on the paddle to keep it from moving.

Because the water is only slightly deflected by the paddle blade, the effect is that of a rudder, only minimally slowing the kayak. Sweeping the paddle out from the kayak in a reverse sweep stroke would also correct the direction, but the kayak would lose too much speed.

Above *The stern rudder. With the upper edge of the blade tilted away from the kayak, the kayak turns towards the paddle (left in this case).*

With the blade upright in the neutral position, the kayak runs straight.

With the upper edge of the blade tilted towards the kayak, the kayak turns to the right, away from the paddle.

Above *Tilting the kayak. The paddler is tilting to his right; his right leg is straightened while the left leg braces.*

The low brace turn

In the low brace turn, the kayak is tilted and the paddle blade ensures balance.

Tilting the kayak

It is possible to tilt a kayak without fear of overturning. As a preparatory exercise, brace yourself with your feet and knees and gently rock the kayak from side to side by lifting one hip and buttock at a time. By bending sideways at the waist you will be able to keep your body upright.

To hold the kayak at a slight tilt, straighten the leg on the side you wish to be lowest, and lift the opposite hip and buttock, bracing upwards with that knee. Keep your body upright, and paddle gently forwards, keeping the kayak at a slight but constant tilt. The water should reach close to the side of your cockpit. Now practise on the opposite side.

The paddle position for the low brace turn

This starts in almost the same position as a stern rudder where the upper edge of the blade is furthest from the kayak, but the paddle blade is held almost flat on the water. As the kayak turns, the blade effectively sweeps in a quarter circle forwards from the stern to a point level with the cockpit (in fact, the paddle blade remains more or less stationary while the kayak turns around it). Hold the elbow of your bottom arm directly above your hand. This is the 'low brace' position. Move your top arm as for a reverse sweep stroke, crossing over the deck of the kayak.

The complete turn

Paddle forwards to build up speed. Tilt the kayak to one side towards the direction you plan to turn, and rest the back of the blade gently on the surface of the water on that side. As your kayak turns, lightly sweep the blade out from the stern and forwards, in the low brace position.

To add polish to the sequence, start it with a forward sweep stroke on the outside of the turn. This will set the kayak turning. Now tilt into the turn and brace lightly as before. With practice this will become a smooth and graceful turn that is almost effortless. The paddle brace will become almost superfluous, as the sweep stroke on the outside of the turn together with the tilt of the kayak will turn you perfectly. The paddle can be useful, however, to maintain your balance, and to bring the kayak around more sharply when required.

If you want to speed up the turn, you can turn more abruptly by beginning the brace beside the cockpit rather than near the stern. This would not be advisable in surf, but is a useful white-water skill.

Right *The low brace turn. Note the tilt of the kayak.*
Below *In the low brace turn the paddle is held nearly flat on the water.*

1

2

3

4

5

6

7

8

9

There are a number of ways in which kayakers can empty an overturned kayak and assist its paddler to re-enter while still in deep water. These are known as *deep-water rescues*. There are also ways of assisting swimmers in difficulty, and of recovering stray kayaks and returning them to the shore.

The 'X' rescue

This is the rescue I personally favour when I need to return the victim of a capsize to their craft with the minimum of fuss and time. It requires only one rescuer, although a second may assist. The rescue is a very stable operation.

1 The victim of a capsize can help enormously by performing a 'clean' capsize – leaving the kayak upside down and undisturbed, taking hold of the end grab and retaining the paddle. If the kayak is unduly disturbed while inverted, it will let in water and be more difficult to empty.

2 As the rescuer, approach the upturned kayak so that you are alongside it, with your bow end grab within easy reach of the person in the water. Take control of the capsized kayak, holding it with one hand. Instruct the swimmer to take hold of your end grab, and *then* to let go of their own. **The swimmer should never be out of physical contact with a kayak**. This is important because the rafted kayaks may be blown away from the swimmer. The wind does not need to be very strong before the kayaks will drift faster than a person can swim, which could be disastrous.

3 Place your own paddle across your lap, beneath your buoyancy aid, where you can grab it should you need it. Float the inverted kayak along until you get a good grip of one end. Now lift the end up and across your front deck (not across your cockpit). This is the time when water may enter the cockpit of the capsized kayak, so make the movement a single quick one to bring the cockpit clear of the water. *Both* hands must hold the cockpit or deck-lines of the upturned kayak, or you will probably lose control of it.

4 With one good body rotation, lift the kayak up and across your deck to the point of balance and 'seesaw' it to drain out the water. If you have mistakenly positioned it across your cockpit, you will be gently reminded of your folly now as the water pours into your own kayak!

5 Now roll the kayak upright on your deck. Its owner should still be holding your bow end grab, and their paddle. Identify the bow of the now empty kayak, and swing it towards your stern, lowering the kayak on to the water beside you.

6 Ask the person at your bow to pass you their paddle. Take care! In my experience the paddle may arrive from any direction, at any angle and at any speed!

7 Now you need to get the swimmer back into the kayak. Lie the two paddles across the kayaks just in front of you, so that they lie across the front deck of the empty kayak just in front of the cockpit. Grip the cockpit firmly to make a tight raft with the other kayak. Clear, concise instructions will make your job easier. Try using the following instructions.

• "Come along between the two kayaks and hold on *here* and *here*." Indicate a point just behind their own cockpit and a point level with it on your own front deck.
• "Lie your head and shoulders back in the water and lift *both feet* into *your* cockpit."
• "Pull the kayaks together behind you and slide on to your

back deck." This stops the swimmer from pushing the kayaks apart, which seems to be the natural thing to do but places enormous strain on the rescuer who is trying desperately to hold them together! Once out of the water and sitting on the back deck,

your companion is likely to wobble a bit, so hold on tightly until they are securely in their seat.

Opposite *The X rescue.*
Below *The standard re-entry from deep water.*

It is important from a safety point of view to be able to rescue a kayaking companion, but equally it is important to do the right things when somebody is rescuing you. It is worth getting wet a few times in practice to save yourself time and anxiety in the water following an accidental capsize.

There are two ways in which you can make the rescue a little easier for yourself, if you find rescuing others heavy going. One way is to call on the assistance of another paddler, who rafts up against you and can lend a hand with lifting the upturned kayak across your deck. The second makes use of the person who is being rescued. If your companion makes their way along the side of your kayak to the cockpit on the opposite side from their own kayak, then as you lift the kayak towards the 'seesaw' position, they can take hold of the end of their own cockpit. Then, by placing their feet on the side or gunwale of your kayak, and slightly straightening their legs

while you lift, they will be able to help in the hardest part of the rescue: pulling the kayak across your deck. You will need to keep a good hold on the cockpit too. If you let go, it is very easy for your assistant to overstretch their legs and pull their kayak away from you into the water again!

I like this second technique. It means that an experienced paddler can coordinate his or her own rescue by a beginner who has never performed a rescue before.

Rescuing a waterlogged kayak

Sooner or later you will come across a kayak so full of water that it is too heavy to empty with the usual 'X' rescue. I can remember grappling with waterlogged kayaks in a desperate bid to haul them across my deck, only to feel my own deck bending on to my legs under the excessive weight. It was a long time before I learned an easier way!

1 Raft up against the waterlogged kayak and ask the person in the water to hold on to your end grab (preferably at the bow) and also their own. They will need to keep their own kayak level.
2 Roll the kayak on its side. The buoyancy in it should float it up in the water, draining out some of the water without you having to lift at all.
3 Take hold of the upper side of the cockpit with both hands and gently lift. Water will pour slowly out of the cockpit. What you are trying to do is to lift the kayak out of the water gradually, leaving the water behind.
4 When the bulk of the water has drained out, ask your companion to lift the end of their kayak over your front deck. As they do this, rotate your body to bring the cockpit you are holding across your deck, and 'seesaw' it empty.

Alternative deep-water rescues

There are alternatives to the 'X' rescue. They involve two rescuers, and so usually take longer to set up, and do have certain disadvantages. However, I think it is a good idea to practise as many different rescues as you can, because kayaking situations vary so much that you need to be versatile.

The 'H' rescue

This rescue requires good positioning and cooperation between two rescuers. It is not easy in choppy water, but offers an excellent method of emptying double kayaks, which can otherwise present you with some puzzling problems!

Each rescuer takes an end of the kayak to be rescued, turning their own kayaks to form the shape of an 'H', with the rescue kayaks at about right angles to the capsized one. The two rescuers together roll the upturned kayak on its side. This makes it easier for them to progressively pull their own kayaks underneath it as the water drains out of the cockpit. The procedure at this stage is similar to that of emptying a waterlogged kayak. When most of the water has drained out, the kayak is rolled upside down, with the bow and stern overlapping the rescue kayaks by about half a metre. Each end is then lifted alternately until the kayak is empty. Then it is righted and manoeuvred into a tight raft between the rescuers ready for re-entry.

Left *Emptying a waterlogged kayak. Most of the water is drained by lifting from the cockpit before finishing here as for an X rescue.*
Right *The H rescue — a tricky rescue, best suited to doubles.*

The Ipswich or 'HI' rescue

This is a tighter formation rescue than the 'H'. The two rescuers raft up either side of the capsized kayak, placing all three paddles across their laps, while the swimmer holds the end grab of a rescue kayak. The upturned kayak is lifted over the paddles until it reaches a balance point, where it can be seesawed across the paddles until empty. The kayak is lifted and turned upright, and eased back on the water again. It is then floated back underneath the paddles and securely held by the rescuers. With this type of rescue, the kayak that has just been emptied may easily be facing the wrong way for its owner to re-enter in the way previously described. It will only be the correct way round if the person in the water has taken the stern end grab rather than the bow one. This should not cause problems; a tight raft of three kayaks should provide enough stability for someone to turn around before sitting down.

The major disadvantage of the 'HI' rescue is that it can easily lead to damage to your paddles – usually abrasions caused by inadvertent dragging of the kayak across the paddle shafts. Scratches in the hand grip areas of a paddle shaft may make it permanently uncomfortable to use. The other damage I have seen is bent paddle shafts, caused by trying to empty a kayak that has too much weight of water in it. Good paddles are not cheap, and I prefer never to use my paddles for this purpose. In all other respects it is a good method of rescue, and one I used frequently myself before I owned my own paddles!

The Ipswich or HI rescue — effective, but it can damage your paddles!

Alternative methods of re-entry

Not everybody finds re-entry from the water between two kayaks the easiest way. Some people find it easier to scramble in over the side, where they can be assisted by the rescuer. Others prefer to pull themselves along the back deck, pushing the stern down between their legs and grabbing the back of the cockpit to give themselves something to pull on. Try the different methods yourself, not just as the person trying to get back into the kayak, but also as the rescuer. Then make up your own mind which method you prefer.

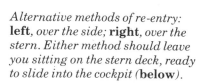

Alternative methods of re-entry: **left**, *over the side;* **right**, *over the stern. Either method should leave you sitting on the stern deck, ready to slide into the cockpit (***below***).*

Above *Rescuing a swimmer: the bow carry.*

A rear-deck carry.

A stern tow.

Towing a kayak.

Assisting a swimmer

I have on a number of occasions been in a position to help other water users: anglers cut off by the tide, or swimmers who have become tired some distance from the shore. Three obvious ways of helping swimmers to shore are described here; you may be able to think of some better ways yourself.
1 Push the swimmer through the water while they cup their hands over the bow of your kayak and keep their head safely on one side. Their body and legs should trail beneath your kayak, keeping out of reach of your paddles.
2 You can carry somebody on your rear deck, if they keep flat and hold your cockpit rim or your deck-line. They will need to grip the sides of your kayak with their legs to avoid sliding off sideways. This method makes you more unstable, and can interfere with your paddle work, but does reduce the drag in the water.
3 You can tow a swimmer who holds on to your end grab. This has the disadvantage that they are not in an easy position for you to talk to or reassure if necessary, but if they are not too tired they can help by kicking their legs and using their free arm, and they are not in a position that would interfere with your paddling.

Below *An 'alongside' or short tow-line tow.*

Towing

Tow-lines are used by kayakers for a variety of retrieval and rescue purposes. In Arctic regions the Inuit have used tow-lines for towing seals and even whales to shore. Here in Britain they are more commonly used for assisting tired paddlers or retrieving a drifting kayak, or for safeguarding deep-water rescues where drifting is undesirable.

Generally, a tow-line will need to be long enough to allow a kayak to be towed without interfering with your stern. It may then be shortened to provide an 'alongside' tow if required. Ideally the tow-line should have a strong clip to fasten to the end grab of the kayak to be towed, a strong line, and a quick-release mechanism to attach to your own kayak or to your body.

I personally prefer to treat my tow-line as a part of my kayaking clothing, so that I always have it available, even if I have changed kayaks partway through a session. I wear a waist belt with a quick-release fastening. To the belt is attached a length of floating line which ends in a stainless steel snap clip. The clip fastens on the belt when not in use, and the line is stored out of the way under my buoyancy aid.

Tow-lines are *not* recommended for use on fast-flowing and white-water rivers: there are alternative rescue techniques for these waters.

This chapter describes strokes with which you can prevent yourself from turning over. A *support stroke* is a stroke that is used to keep yourself in balance, in an upright or leaning position; *recovery strokes* are used to bring yourself to a stable position whenever you lose your balance; and *sculling* is a continuous paddle movement that may be adapted for maintaining balance or for drawing the kayak sideways.

When you practise these strokes, the side of the cockpit will often dip beneath the water, so you will need to wear a *spray-deck*. A spray-deck is usually made of waterproof nylon material, which seals around your waist and around the cockpit rim with elastic.

The spray-deck must have a *release strap* which should be easy to find, even when you are upside down. The release strap will enable you to lift the elastic from behind the cockpit rim. The spray-deck is worn like a skirt. I usually fasten it to the cockpit rim starting at the back and working around to the front. Have a few 'dry runs' to see how it is best put on and to see how the release strap works. Ease the elastic from behind the cockpit rim rather than pulling hard on the release strap, and then run your fingers around inside the deck to release the elastic all the way round the cockpit before you get out. The whole procedure of removing the spray-deck only takes a few seconds, and is the first stage of getting out following a capsize.

Whenever you fasten your spray-deck, check that your release strap is on the outside where you can reach it. It is easy to forget and to seal the strap beneath the spray-deck, which can perplex you a little if you try to find it underwater! If you ever find yourself in this predicament, lean to one side, grab hold of the slack material that will gather by your hip and lift the elastic out using this.

A spray-deck is essential equipment for sea or white-water kayaking, and for Eskimo rolling. It is a good idea to practise a capsize when you first wear a spray-deck on the water, so that you are completely familiar with the exit procedure before you progress further.

Fastening a spray-deck. Starting at the back, work around the sides to the front. Finally, check it is on correctly.

Above *The spray-deck is worn around the waist like a skirt.*

Releasing a spray-deck. Ease the elastic from behind the cockpit rim using the release strap.

Releasing a spray-deck from the side. A good, foolproof method.

Support strokes

There are two blade presentations used for support strokes. One uses the back of the blade – the *low brace position*. The elbow is held directly above the paddle shaft and the hand pushes down on the shaft; your weight is above your paddle. The other uses the drive face of the blade and is called the *high brace position*. The elbow is below the paddle shaft and the hand pulls down.

The low brace position is the best for maintaining balance when you feel slightly unstable. If you start to tilt your kayak, the low brace stroke can be used until just beyond the point at which you lose your balance.

If you sit on the floor in the low brace position with your elbow above your hand, you will discover that you cannot lean very far over to that side, and still push yourself upright again easily. This is where the high brace position is most useful. Because your arm is beneath the paddle and is pulling down, the high brace can be used even when you are under the water. It is, in fact, the basis of an Eskimo roll.

To use the low brace for stability when you are moving, rest the paddle blade on the water, level with your cockpit, with the leading edge of the blade slightly raised to keep it on the surface. A slight tilt towards your paddle will ensure that you do not lose balance in either direction. A support stroke of this kind is often used by kayakers when they want to have a good look behind them, especially if they are in a 'tippy' kayak.

Below *Two blade presentations for support strokes.* **Top** *Low brace position.* **Bottom** *High brace position.*

Recovery strokes

Low brace position

Get into the low brace position. Now tilt your kayak to its point of balance by lifting one buttock and knee, keeping your body as upright as you can. Your stroke-side leg should be straight to help you hold this position. Hold your paddle just above the water. Whenever you lose your balance, immediately press down on the water with your paddle and sharply raise your stroke-side knee to right your kayak. Because you are only just going off balance each time, it is very easy to recover your balance again, so this is an excellent exercise to practise. Alternate your practice between one side and the other.

Below *The low brace recovery stroke.*

High brace position

Now try the high brace position. Raise your paddle to shoulder height and drop your elbow beneath your paddle shaft. You are now in the position you might adopt if you were going to perform some chin-ups on a bar, and in fact the movement you use is similar, although you will only use one hand.

Tilt your kayak to the point of balance once more. Hold your paddle blade at shoulder height above the water, and bring your other hand as low as possible, touching the side of your cockpit. By keeping your non-active hand as low as possible, your working blade will be as close to being flat on the water as you can get it, providing you with the maximum support. As you lose balance, pull down on the paddle, while raising your knee in the same way as before.

Alternate your practice from one side to the other. You will probably find it harder to keep your non-active hand low when you are practising on your non-control side. This is perfectly normal.

Once you feel happy with the stroke, allow yourself to fall further and further out of balance before you begin your recovery stroke. Then practise sculling for support, because this will also improve your high brace support strokes.

1

2

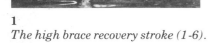

3

The high brace recovery stroke (1-6).

4

5

6

Recovering on the move. If balance is lost at the end of a paddle stroke, recover using a low brace support stroke.

Sculling for support

Low brace position

Get into the low brace position, with your paddle blade resting on the water to one side. Gently push the blade forwards, lifting the leading edge slightly to stop the blade from diving. Now bring the blade gently back again with the new leading edge raised to prevent it from diving. This is the 'sculling' movement. For good support, you will need to restrict your sculling to the middle 45 degrees of the possible semicircle, keeping the blade away from the bow and stern.

Tilt your kayak to its balance point and start sculling. You should now be able to tilt a little further and yet still be in control by sculling. Remember that in the low brace position there is a limit to how far you can lean and still keep control, so do not lean too far!

Sculling for support in the low brace position is often used by paddlers in tippy kayaks such as racing kayaks to maintain their stability when they are stationary. It is also used on white water and in surf.

Below *Sculling for support in the low brace position.*

If balance is lost at the start of a paddle stroke, use a high brace stroke to recover.

High brace position

Sculling for support in the high brace position uses the same blade movement as low brace sculling, but the drive face of the blade is used and the elbow is beneath the paddle instead of above it.

Tilt your kayak to its point of balance and then support yourself just beyond the balance point by sculling. Your paddle shaft should remain as horizontal as possible. Now bend your neck back so that the back of your head is as close to the water as possible, and twist your body so that your back is to the water. This is the correct position for lowering yourself still further. However, we will change to a different exercise first to practise this position.

For this exercise you will need to make use of another kayak, or a low jetty, or persuade a companion to stand in the water to support your paddle blade at water level. Keeping your kayak as upright as possible, lower your body level with the cockpit, supporting yourself on your paddle in the high brace position, until you are lying on the water. Now twist your body until your back is almost flat on the water, and turn your head so that the back of your head is in the water and you are looking directly upwards. This is the body position I want you to adopt to practise your sculling.

To come upright from this position, pull down on the paddle and flick your kayak upright by bringing your stroke-side armpit towards your hip, at the same time lifting that hip and thigh. Practise this manoeuvre on alternate sides of the kayak.

When you have mastered the 'righting' procedure, and can drop effortlessly into the correct body position on either side, ask your companion to help you by holding the kayak to prevent it from capsizing while you practise your sculling with the body position just described. You will then be able to relax into the correct position without fear of capsizing, look up at the sky and concentrate on sculling. While you scull, adjust the angle of your kayak constantly by moving your hips and knees, and right yourself frequently. Your companion may assist to start with if you find it difficult, but once you get the sculling and righting movements correct, you will be able to feel the smoothness and relative effortlessness of the stroke. Your companion can then let you get on with it by yourself, standing ready in case you should need a hand. Remember to alternate from side to side.

Once you have mastered sculling for support in the high brace position, you will find the high brace recovery stroke much easier. Both techniques are essential stepping stones towards the Eskimo roll.

Below *The body position for sculling for support in the high brace position.*

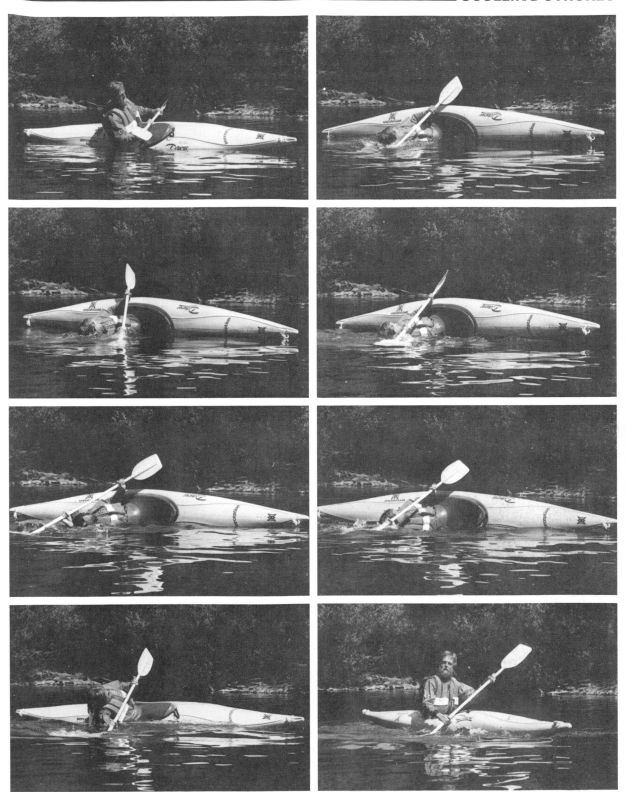

Sculling for support in the high brace position.

The sculling draw

Above *The sculling draw, with near-vertical paddle.*

The sculling draw uses a near-vertical paddle, so that the blade is on end and deep in the water, as for the draw stroke described in Chapter 6. The drive face is towards the kayak, and as the blade is guided forwards and backwards roughly parallel to the kayak, the leading edge is held further from the kayak than the trailing edge. It is this that pulls you sideways through the water. In order to maintain a constant pull on the paddle, even when the paddle is changing direction, the blade is pulled *in* towards the kayak at the end of each stroke, and is guided slightly *out* from the kayak during each stroke – thus making a figure-of-eight alongside the kayak.

The kayak is held upright for this stroke, or with the leading side of the kayak very slightly raised, and in order to twist the body to face the direction of travel, the knee on the side of the stroke is raised, while the other leg is straightened to press against the footrest.

You will find that by increasing the angle of the blade from the side of the kayak, you will make the kayak turn. For example, if you bring the blade towards the bow with a small angle, and towards the stern with a larger angle, the stern will move sideways more quickly than the bow and the kayak will turn.

You might like to try altering the angle of the blade so that the leading edge is closer to your kayak than the trailing edge; this will push your kayak across the water rather than pulling it.

Photo: Tickle Design Group.

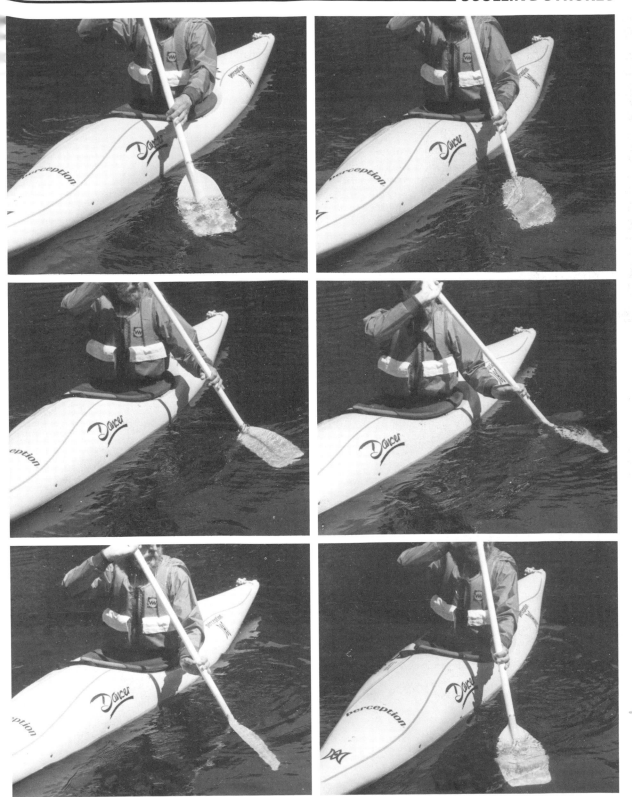

The sculling draw; note the figure-of-eight paddle movement.

10 The bow rudder turn and hanging draw

The bow rudder turn

The bow rudder turn is a satisfyingly precise turn that ends with the kayak moving forwards in a straight line. It is a stroke commonly used by white-water and slalom paddlers for crossing into and out of eddies, and its appearance of effortless fluency makes it a popular technique for learners. Fortunately it is not a complicated technique. It is a logical progression from the draw stroke and the sculling draw. It is best learned in stages.

The basic turn

1 Begin with the paddle in the starting position for a draw stroke. The body should be twisted towards the paddle, your paddle-side leg should be straight and your other knee should be raised, and your top hand should be almost directly above your bottom hand.
2 Angle your blade towards your feet and draw it in that direction. Your kayak should turn towards your paddle.
3 When your paddle nears your feet, adjust the angle of the blade gradually in a curve until the drive face is towards you.
4 Finish by pulling the paddle towards you in a forward paddle stroke close to the kayak.

This change in the angle of the blade is very similar to that used in the sculling draw, as there should be a pull against the water all the way around. The effect of the stroke so far should be to draw the bow round to point in a new direction, and to propel the kayak forwards while stopping it from turning further. Remember to practise on both sides.

Improving the turn

Paddle forwards to pick up some speed, and repeat the sequence above, tilting your kayak towards your paddle while you turn. You will find the turn is now more powerful and effective. The forward power stroke at the end of the turn should be just enough to stop the kayak from turning further, and not powerful enough to start it turning in the opposite direction.

To improve the turn still further, begin the sequence with a forward sweep on the outside of the turn. So, the sequence is now:

1 Paddle forwards in a straight line.
2 Start the turn with a sweep stroke on the outside.
3 Continue the turn with a draw stroke towards your feet, which then curves around into . . .
4 a forward paddle stroke, which finishes the turn and propels you in your new direction.

With a manoeuvrable kayak, the paddle may be placed upright in the water alongside the cockpit, as with a sculling draw stroke, with the front edge of the blade angled away from the kayak. In this position the elbow of your bottom arm will be tucked in towards your hip, and both elbows will be bent at about right angles. This will give you a very strong hold on the paddle. The paddle blade is turned in a much smaller area beside the kayak, yet the change in angle of the blade is exactly the same as before. The result is a tighter, sharper turn at speed.

If we look at what happens to the paddle during this turn, we find that the blade stays more or less in the same position, and at the same blade angle relative to the surroundings, while the kayak circles around it.

Finally, try blending a low brace turn with a bow rudder turn. Pick up forward speed to start with, then sweep forwards to begin the turn. Follow this with a low brace stroke from the stern on the inside of the turn, and as your paddle blade reaches a point roughly level with your cockpit, push your top arm across your kayak to bring your paddle upright in the water. Rotate the paddle to direct the drive face towards your feet, and smoothly continue your turn with a bow rudder turn.

Blending one stroke into another in this way will help you develop the fluency that is the hallmark of a competent paddler.

Photo: Tickle Design Group.

The bow rudder turn.

The hanging draw

The 'hanging draw' is a variation on the use of a draw stroke in the sculling position. It is performed at speed to draw the kayak sideways across the water without turning it. The paddle is used in the water with the drive face 'open' a little towards the bow – that is, with the leading edge of the blade slightly further from the kayak than the trailing edge, as in a sculling draw.

Remember how a draw stroke towards the *back* of your cockpit pulls the stern of your kayak sideways more quickly than the bow, and a draw stroke towards the *front* of your cockpit draws the bow sideways more quickly than the stern? Well, the hanging draw makes use of this.

Start with your paddle as upright in the water as possible, and with the blade a little behind your cockpit to one side. You will need to rotate your body well to get into this position. To begin with, hold the blade parallel to the kayak, so that it is in a neutral position.

Now gently 'open' the blade towards the bow until it is at about 45 degrees from the line of the kayak. At this point, if you were moving forwards across the water, the stern would be drawn towards the paddle; however, you want to keep the kayak parallel to its original course, so gently move the paddle forwards. The stern will be moving sideways, and you need to match this by drawing the bow sideways too. Guide the blade further and further forwards, until by the time your kayak has lost most of its speed, your blade will be level with your knee or your foot.

Now use the stroke at speed. During the first few attempts, most people seem to turn towards their paddles; if this happens, begin the stroke nearer to the stern, or move the paddle forwards more slowly. Do not be discouraged! It is a subtle skill, and one that baffles many paddlers. Persevere until you have cracked it and it will give you a good deal of satisfaction.

With practice you will be able to hold the blade in a single position to perform the hanging draw, rather than needing to move it to retain control, and will be able to use a variety of different paddle positions to do this.

I use the hanging draw most frequently when I find myself paddling too close alongside another kayak, or when I want to avoid a rock or other obstacle that has suddenly appeared in my path, without changing my direction. It is also a perfect way of gliding sideways into a jetty using what remains of your forward speed.

Below *The hanging draw.*

The bow rudder turn demonstrated by world champion Richard Fox (photo: Tickle Design Group).

11 The Eskimo roll

Now we come to one of the most magical kayaking skills, the Eskimo roll. This is a self-righting technique developed by the Eskimos to help them survive in their kayaks in the Arctic. Although various techniques were described by many of the earliest Arctic explorers, it was not until 1927 that a man called H. W. Pawlata, after studying written descriptions of the Eskimo techniques, became the first European to roll a kayak. Kayaking has come a long way since then, yet I doubt there is a single type of roll that we use nowadays that was not previously used by the Eskimos.

Rolling is a useful technique for any paddler to learn. It increases paddle, body and spatial awareness, and it saves time and effort after those embarrassing momentary lapses of concentration that occasionally leave you upside down! Rolling is also an important skill for those venturing on the sea, or down white-water rivers, where the elements play a greater part in overturning you.

The Eskimo roll has two components: a body movement and a paddle movement. Each can be practised in isolation, and in fact the body movement when performed well can enable you to roll up using your hand instead of the paddle.

The body movement

There are two alternative body movements used in rolling, the *hip flick* and the *lie back*. However, as with so many kayaking skills, there are hybrids which incorporate a bit of each. The hip flick is the best method in white water, because the paddler completes the roll sitting up. The lie back, on the other hand, ends with the paddler lying on the back deck, which is not a good position to be in if you need to respond quickly to the vagaries of the rough water. The lie back does have the advantage of keeping your centre of gravity very low, enabling you to roll up gradually and with very little effort.

The hip flick

The hip flick consists of the upward jerk of one hip towards the armpit as described for the high recovery stroke. This action can be practised on land. Sit upright on the ground with your legs in front of you, as if you were sitting in a kayak. Now lean over to one side and put your elbow on the ground about the length of your forearm from your hip. Roll your legs with your knees together until the side of your knee touches the ground. Now jerk your backside back into a sitting position, keeping your elbow on the ground and dropping your head until your cheek rests close to your shoulder. This is the hip flick that rights your kayak, after which you can bring your body upright.

Below *Practising the hip flick on dry land. The top row shows the body movement; the bottom row shows the same sequence in a kayak.*

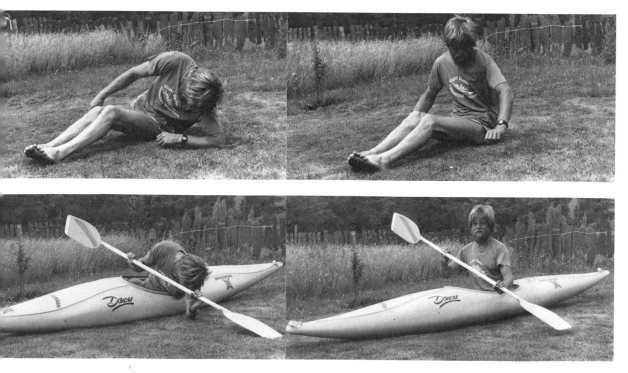

The lie back. Capsize in an upright or leaning forward body position (1, 2).

3 Rotate body to bring chest uppermost and right kayak.

4 Bring body round on to rear deck.

5, 6 Finally, bring body upright again.

Below *The Eskimo rescue.*

The lie back

When you are upside down in your kayak, lean forwards to one side, so that the flotation in your buoyancy aid will help to bring you close to the surface. As you first pull down on your paddle, start to rotate your body so as to bring your chest to the surface while bringing your hip towards your armpit. The movement of your hip rights the kayak, and should leave you lying on your back on the water with your body at about right angles to the kayak. To complete the movement, continue to pull down on your paddle to bring your body on to the back deck, with the back of your head leaving the water last.

The Eskimo rescue

The Eskimo rescue is a useful safety net when you are learning to roll. If you need help when you are upside down, bang your hands sharply on the hull of the kayak to attract attention, then keep one hand up on each side of the kayak and wait. If your companion then comes *carefully* alongside, taking hold of the end of your kayak for control, and gently touches your hand with their bow, you will be able to grip the bow and pull up on it, using a hip flick or a lie back to right your kayak. Once you have mastered the Eskimo rescue, you can be sure of staying in your kayak even if you fail a roll.

Hands banged on hull and then held up to attract attention. The rescuer takes hold of the end of upturned kayak to stop, and very carefully eases bow into a waiting hand. Kayak is righted with hip flick or lie back.

Learning the screw roll with a helper. Topple away from your paddle until your body hits the water. Your helper can support you in this position by holding the rear deck. Scull the paddle round and use a hip flick or lie back to right the kayak.

The screw roll and put-across roll

These are probably the most useful rolls to learn first. They will serve you well in whatever branch of the sport you may follow in the future.

The screw roll

Hold your paddle in the stern rudder position with the upper edge of the blade tilted away from the kayak. Now lean forwards and push the paddle well forwards. This is the starting position for the roll (often called the 'wind-up'). Before you capsize, guide the front blade out about 30 cm (1 ft) from the kayak, and the rear blade underneath your hull. You will need to do this normally when you are upside down, to ensure that your back blade clears your kayak as you roll.

Now allow yourself to topple over to the side away from your paddle. As your body hits the water, scull your blade round and use either a hip flick or a lie back to right your craft. To maximize the efficiency of the blade, scull it forwards again when it reaches an angle of about 45 degrees behind you. This is useful because the closer your blade gets to the boat, the less leverage you will get from it. By bringing the blade forwards again, it passes back in to the area of maximum leverage, level with your body, so if you failed to get completely up in the first attempt, you will get another chance.

Continue this exercise on both sides until you are able to drop completely upside down before rolling up; you are now only one step away from a complete roll. You will by now have got the feel of the roll and it only remains for you to capsize towards your paddles so that you fall in on one side and come up again on the opposite side.

Above *The starting (wind-up) position for the screw roll.*

The screw roll. The body is leaned towards the paddle, which is lifted clear of the water. The rear blade is carried across the hull as the front blade is sculled from bow to stern. For extra power and control, scull the blade forwards once more from stern towards the bow.

When you practise, have a companion standing in the water alongside your rear deck, ready to grip your boat and help right it if you need any assistance.

The put-across roll

Start in the screw roll wind-up position. Bring your paddle around until it is at right angles to your kayak, with the paddle shaft extending across the hull of your kayak. This is the starting position for the put-across roll. Push the blade up to the surface, leaning forwards and to the surface on that side as you do so, and then pull directly down on the paddle to right yourself.

If you start a put-across from the screw roll position, which is not essential, you can proceed as for a screw roll by sculling the blade round into the put-across position, and benefit from the extra paddle power. This hybrid roll is quite popular and is often affectionately called a 'screw-across'.

Suggestions for practice

1 Always lean your body towards the surface before you begin your roll. This saves the effort of dragging your body through the water during the roll itself.
2 If your roll is not completely successful, attempt to retrieve the situation using a recovery stroke.
3 If your rolling starts to get worse rather than better, take a break, and go back to practising your body movement without your paddles; then ask somebody to support your kayak so that you can concentrate on perfecting your paddle movement.

4 It can be very helpful to rehearse the roll in your mind whenever you have a quiet moment. I sometimes suggest people think it through in bed and then sleep on it.

5 As soon as you have mastered the roll, practise in as many different situations as possible. This will make you more adaptable and improve your confidence for the time when you capsize accidentally.

The put-across roll. Moving the paddle into the starting position.

The roll, with hip flick.

A look at some other rolls

There are four basic paddle movements that can be used in an Eskimo roll, but minor variations on these have produced a much larger number of identifiable rolls. The four paddle movements all resemble strokes you are already familiar with.

High brace recovery

The high brace recovery is the basis of the put-across roll, which can also be performed with an extended paddle.

Sculling for support

Sculling for support forms the basis of the screw and the reverse screw rolls. In the reverse screw the blade is sculled from the stern towards the bow. These two rolls may be performed with the paddle extended to provide extra leverage, in which case they are called the Pawlata and (in reverse) the steyr. It is also possible to scull oneself upright gradually, using a continuous sculling action.

Forward paddle stroke

The forward paddle stroke is the basis of the storm roll. This requires a vigorous hip flick, and starts as for a screw roll. Instead of a paddle sweep across the surface, the blade is pulled deep alongside the kayak. The storm roll is effective in aerated water because the blade grips the deeper water which is less frothy than the surface water. It also has the effect of propelling the kayak forwards.

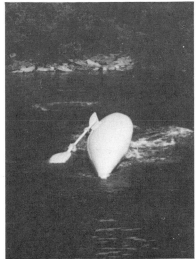

Right *The storm roll, which uses an action similar to a forward pulling stroke.*

Draw stroke

The draw stroke when performed underwater gives the leverage for the vertical paddle roll. Like the storm roll, this is a useful roll in aerated water, reaching deep into the currents flowing beneath the surface. Like the storm roll, it requires a powerful hip flick.

Right and below *The vertical paddle roll uses a paddle action similar to a draw stroke.*

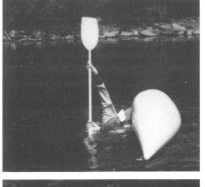

Below *A screw roll using a sea kayak.*

The selection of equipment is very much a matter for personal choice; the information in this chapter will help you decide what is right for you.

Clothing

Keeping yourself comfortable in warm climates is no great problem, although you may need protection against the glare of the sun on the water, which can burn you in unexpected places such as beneath the chin and under the eyebrows. A hat with a brim or peak, sunglasses and a long-sleeved shirt will often be sufficient.

In cooler climates the combination of low temperatures, cold water and a breeze will rapidly chill an inadequately clad paddler. The most common outfits are as follows:

1 A wet suit long-john without arms, worn with a sweater of wool or fibre-pile and topped with a waterproof cagoule or anorak.
2 A thermal suit of fibre-pile, or a sweater and trousers, covered with a cagoule and waterproof overtrousers.
3 A dry suit, worn over a thermal suit or a sweater and warm trousers.

A buoyancy aid and suitable footwear should also be worn, together with a spray-deck and helmet where appropriate.

Wet suits

Wet suits are a popular choice for paddlers involved in the wetter branches of kayaking, such as white-water and kayak surfing. They are made of flexible neoprene, which contains tiny trapped air bubbles. It is these bubbles that make neoprene such a good insulator, and incidentally make it buoyant. Thicknesses of 3 mm to 4 mm are usually used for kayaking suits. Wet suits insulate whether wet or dry, but need to be

close-fitting to perform properly. The long-john style, covering the trunk and legs, and cut deep at the armpit to allow the shoulder and arm full mobility, is the most popular style for kayaking. Long-johns may have a front zip or Velcro shoulder fastenings, and ankle zips for ease of access. Men will find a two-way front zip a welcome convenience. Lining materials range from nylon and Lycra to towelling. Lycra is toughest and is often used on the outside of a suit.

When trying on a wet suit, look for a snug fit and ease of arm movement, and do sit down in it to make sure it is comfortable when you are in a paddling position. What may seem a comfortably tight suit when you are standing up may prove too tight over the shoulders and in the crutch when you sit down. Kayaking wet suits are commonly made of 3 mm thick neoprene as it gives good freedom of movement, but a well-designed suit will have thicker neoprene on the knees and the seat – the areas that receive the greatest punishment.

Cagoules or anoraks

These are short, waterproof garments which reach down to the waist and are produced in a variety of materials, designs and colours. There should be plenty of room at the armpit, yet the sleeves, particularly below the elbow, should not be too baggy. Move your arms in all directions to check for freedom of movement. If in doubt, choose a different design, or go for a larger size. Cheaper cags generally have seams that are merely stitched. Ideally they should be glued and stitched, welded or taped over. Collars are frequently fastened with Velcro. Open the collar to make sure that there is a fold of material inside to prevent water pouring in if the neck is open. Cuffs are usually sealed with elastic, Velcro, or are

made of neoprene (neoprene is probably warmest). Pockets in cags can be useful, particularly for sea kayaking, but there is a limit to what you can comfortably carry in this way.

For maximum water resistance, 'dry cags' are the answer. These combine watertight seams with latex rubber seals around the neck and wrists. They are excellent garments for cold-weather paddling and are especially comforting in wet weather and in rough water, when a slight dampness inside the cuffs and neck is the worst you need expect after a day's paddling. However, they are not very comfortable in hot weather, as there is no way of letting out excess heat.

'Dry cags' have a looser seal around the waist, and water will seep upwards from the waist if you immerse yourself in water. The neck and wrist seals do need to be handled with care, and will suffer damage in excessive heat, but they can be easily replaced by the manufacturers if they become damaged. When you buy a dry cag or suit, the wrist and neck seals will need to be trimmed down to fit you. The first time I tried one on for size I thought my eyes were going to pop out, the neck was so tight! They are quite comfortable once they have been customized.

Dry suits

If you paddle regularly in cold conditions, you might consider a full dry suit. Latex rubber seals at the neck, wrists and ankles keep out the water; entry and exit from the suit is through a special waterproof zip across the back. Dry suits are normally worn over warm clothing. A one-piece, fibre-pile thermal suit is a popular undergarment as it cannot come apart at the waist to cause discomfort in a place that is inaccessible once you are sealed inside the dry suit. The lighter-weight dry suits designed for boardsailing and dinghy sailing are more suitable for kayaking than the heavier and more expensive ones intended for diving.

A major drawback for the paddler is that a dry suit is cumbersome to remove if nature calls. A suit constructed in two pieces is available; the top and bottom roll together to provide the required seal, yet they may be worn separately, or peeled apart when necessary.

Clothing. 1 basic cagoule, 2 dry cag, 3 basic buoyancy aid, 4 buoyancy aid with pockets, 5 toddler's buoyancy aid, 6 twin-seal spray-deck, 7 neoprene spray-deck, 8 nylon spray-deck, 9 wet-suit long john, 10 wet-suit boots, 11 lightweight helmet, 12-14 full weight helmets.

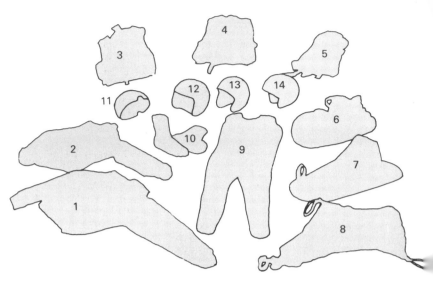

Buoyancy aids or personal flotation devices

The most basic style of PFD pulls over the head and fastens around the waist, is of a waistcoat shape and has a buoyancy of 6 kg (13 lb). Others have a front zip or tapes and buckles to fasten at the front, and some have useful pockets, but they all serve the same purpose of keeping you afloat.

The main styles incorporate either slabs of buoyant foam front and back, or a number of ribs of foam. The slab type is simplest to produce and consequently tends to be cheaper, while the ribbed type allows a little more freedom of movement. Designs for white water often incorporate a full harness with attachment points for rescue purposes.

Lifejackets are also used, although less commonly nowadays. They have a slab of buoyancy on the chest and a further ring around the neck, and when fully inflated to a buoyancy of 16 kg (35 lb) are designed to turn the wearer face up in the water. However, the jacket is too cumbersome for paddling in its inflated state, and is worn deflated to a buoyancy of about 6 kg (13 lb). Lifejackets do not offer the same degree of body protection as buoyancy aids, and are not normally recommended for use where there is a risk of collision. This includes kayaking in white water or surf, and games such as canoe polo. However, lifejackets are well suited for open water expeditions where there is a risk of spending a long time in the water.

Footwear

Wet-suit boots are ideal for cold weather. I look for a sturdy but flexible sole that will give protection for my feet when I scramble around on rocky shores, as well as protecting against unseen objects under water. When I sit in my kayak, the soles of my feet are in contact with my footrest, but my heels are also touching the floor, so the sole needs to continue around the heel to prevent the neoprene of the boot wearing through. Wet-suit boots need to fit well to be effective. A loose boot will fill with water and will not be very warm. If one size is too small and the next a little large, you can wear a pair of socks to get a better fit.

Neoprene socks worn inside plastic sandals make a good combination. The socks alone will give little protection to your soles and will wear out very quickly. In summer, a pair of plastic sandals with a pair of ordinary socks will be quite adequate. Ordinary running shoes are fine, but they will disintegrate quickly with regular use in water.

Spray-decks

Spray-decks can make paddling far more enjoyable, by keeping water out of your cockpit; some achieve this better than others. A spray-deck should be comfortably tight around your waist to prevent water from entering here, and should fit securely around your cockpit. You should be able to lean forwards, backwards and sideways without it coming free. If it releases when you perform a hip flick, it will be of limited use to you. There should be a minimum of bagging over your lap and behind you, otherwise water will collect in these areas. A strap over the shoulder can prevent the waist of the deck being dragged down and inverting under the weight of water.

One of the most irritating faults in spray-decks is leaking seams. A seam that is stitched but not glued or taped is almost certainly going to leak. Have a close look at all the seams. Welded seams are fine.

Latex rubber spray-decks are shaped in one piece, so they have no seams, but the material needs careful handling. They have the advantage of remaining tight across your lap and preventing a pool of water gathering there, as do neoprene decks and the 'twin seal' type which sandwiches a layer of closed cell foam between two layers of nylon across your lap. Some designs are desperately difficult to fit around the cockpit, and will cause you frustration if you have cold hands.

Nylon decks are the cheapest and most common. Neoprene proofing on the nylon seems to last much better than other proofings. Nylon adjustable spray-decks can be made to fit a range of cockpit sizes, and are good general-purpose decks.

Protection for the head

A great deal of body heat can be lost by the head, so a woolly hat or balaclava is a sensible addition to your winter clothing. Whenever you are at risk of hitting your head, especially in white-water kayaking, surfing and coastal 'rock dodging', wear a helmet. Modern white-water helmets are comfortable and warm, often being extensively padded within a protective shell of glass-reinforced plastic (GRP). Look for a helmet that fits well, does not hurt your ears and that protects as much of your head as possible.

Pogies

Hands are best kept warm inside pogies, which are simple gauntlets that fasten on to the paddle shaft. Your hands grasp the paddle shaft as normal, but are protected from the worst of the elements. Pogies are usually made from waterproof nylon, but are available with fleecy linings for extra warmth and comfort. Look for pogies with a wrist opening wide enough to let you slip your hands in and out easily; stiffening in the material in this area will help. Try the pogies on a paddle to make sure there is sufficient room for you to open your fingers for forward paddling.

Kayaks

There is a wide choice of specialist kayaks. Many people start with a general-purpose kayak, then move on to one of the specialist craft described below.

Touring kayak

These are designed with only placid water in mind. They tend to be straight-running kayaks with large, open cockpits, and they are usually stable. They make good beginner's boats because they are easy to get in and out of. They are ideal for inland touring on canals, placid rivers and lakes, and as a kayak to start in if you wish to progress into sprint racing. They are not suitable for white water of grade III or above, sea or surf.

The placid-water touring kayak has a straight keel, with little or no rocker (uplifting of the keel towards the bow and stern), and features a cutting bow. Materials do not need to be exceptionally strong, so lightweight glass-reinforced plastic (GRP) or cheaper grades of thermoplastic are perfectly adequate. This results in a kayak that is not too demanding on the pocket!

Sprint kayak

The sprint kayak is a logical development from the placid-water touring kayak. It has the same straight keel and large cockpit, but to make it faster, the length is increased while the beam is decreased. The smaller the wetted surface area of the hull, the less drag there will be, so the main part of the hull approaches a semicircle in cross-section. The narrow beam and semicircular hull cross-section make this type of craft 'tippy'. It is best to start racing in a placid-water touring kayak, or a less extreme racing design, and to progress towards the faster designs.

A small rudder is added for

Top *Touring kayak.* **Centre** *Sprint kayak with over-stern rudder.*
Bottom *White-water touring kayaks; the one on the right is a 'bat'.*

steering which is controlled by a tiller between the feet. In order to conform to a minimum width restriction imposed for competition, the deck behind the paddler overhangs the water, while the deck in front of the paddler is kept as narrow as possible to allow the paddle blades to enter the water close to the centre line of the kayak.

Sprint racing is an Olympic sport.

White-water touring kayak

White-water touring kayaks come in many shapes and sizes. Generally, they are short, highly rockered and stable. Modern designs have large cockpits for a quick emergency exit, but unlike the cockpit of the sprint and placid-water touring craft there are shaped grips for the thighs to permit greater control. In handling, the short, highly rockered, stable hull makes a very manoeuvrable kayak, slower in a straight line than a placid-water tourer, but much faster to turn. It is a suitable kayak for all white-water conditions on rivers and on the sea, and also for close coastal exploration and surfing. In order to withstand the knocks associated with rough-water paddling, these kayaks are built to high specifications, from tough, impact-absorbing plastics or strengthened GRP, often with the addition of tough laminates of Diolen, Kevlar or carbon fibre. The cockpit region is strengthened internally to resist any pressure that might collapse the kayak on to the paddler's legs. The buoyancy inside is kept to a maximum. Protective bow caps are common, and for the heaviest water, internal cockpit cages are fitted. Gunwales tend to be rounded so that there are no sharp edges to catch in the water.

Some white-water kayaks are very short, being of particular use to paddlers attempting rocky mountain streams, or seeking greater entertainment in heavy water, but the higher-volume, longer designs make better general purpose kayaks, and may be fitted with a detachable skeg to make the kayak run much straighter. Longer kayaks are suitable for beginners, and are also used by experts for major self-sufficient white-water expeditions. These longer designs developed from slalom kayaks of the late 1960s and early 1970s; the shorter designs originated from kayaks intended for swimming-pool training, and later used for canoe polo competition. These shorter kayaks are known as 'bats'.

Sea kayaks

Sea kayaks are intended for sea touring, although they are also used on lakes and gentle rivers. A straight keel line with little rocker and a long hull give the sea kayak its directional stability. However, there has to be a compromise between the degree of tippiness and the directional stability; the flatter the hull, the more stable it feels to sit in, but the less directionally stable it becomes. The bow is usually of a cutting type and is buoyant if the paddler is to be kept dry in rough conditions. Designed primarily for straight running, the sea kayak provides a means of rapid travel, enabling the paddler to cover long distances with relatively little effort.

Modern designs have carrying capacity for long self-sufficient expeditions, and camping equipment can be loaded through hatches into watertight compartments. To aid rescues with laden kayaks and to keep the cockpit dry during long periods afloat, pumps are commonly fitted to the footrest or to the deck. Because of the straight-running nature of sea kayaks, they are normally tilted to turn, although in some cases rudders are fitted.

Below *Sea kayak.*

Slalom kayak

The slalom kayak is a stable, highly manoeuvrable craft with a high degree of rocker. The hull is fairly flat in cross-section and there is little space between the hull and the deck, which are flattened together. The cockpit is large in order to allow the paddler to squeeze in. If this design is not conducive to comfort, the slalom competitor may gain consolation from the fact that slalom courses are short and quickly completed!

Competition rules stipulate a minimum length and beam for a competing kayak. The course is marked out by a series of 'gates', comprising poles hung above the water, between which the competitors must manoeuvre their craft. Penalties are incurred for touching a pole. As a result of the rules, the design of slalom kayaks changed from a high-volume white-water kayak to a craft that was so low on the water that it could slip beneath a pole without touching it, enabling sharper turns to be made into and out of gates. Once these low-line kayaks appeared, paddlers discovered that they could be sliced beneath the surface deliberately to avoid the poles, and the decks were then modified to allow more underwater control. At the same time, it was considered that the ideal handling length for competition was shorter than the minimum allowed. This was overcome by designing a shorter kayak and adding a short pole or spike to the end, to bring the kayak to the required length. Unfortunately there have been some horrific accidents where people have been skewered by the sharp bows of slalom kayaks, so this type of kayak is only really suitable for slalom competition, and is not a wise choice for general recreation. Slalom competition is, however, a good way to develop accuracy and economy of strokework on moving water, and provides white-water fun and motivation where the choice of good paddling water is limited.

Squirt kayak

This is a kayak designed to 'squirt' from the water in the same way as an orange pip might squirt from between your fingers. The name is no reflection on the type of person who uses these craft! The squirt boat developed from the slalom kayak, initially by the simple amputation of the unnecessary pointed ends that keep the slalom kayak to the length required for competition. The resulting craft is a short, high-performance fun boat with the same dipping characteristics as a slalom kayak. Development from this starting point has been to spoon (make concave) the front and stern decks, and to cut down on the overall buoyancy of the kayak to a point where it may be sliced completely underwater. The product of these modifications is a kayak that is easily looped end over end and pirouetted even on flat water, and which in expert hands will cavort on, in and under white water in a fluid, three-dimensional dance, making use of water currents beneath the surface that other kayaks cannot reach. The squirt boat is a challenging fun craft with great potential.

Slalom kayak (photo: Tickle Design Group).

White-water racing kayak

White-water racing kayaks are straight-running kayaks designed for paddling down white-water rivers at speed. They have a high buoyancy to keep them on the surface in the aerated water, a cutting bow and little or no rocker. The hull is normally 'fish-form' like a sprint kayak, and like the sprint kayak, the widest point in the deck is above the waterline and behind the paddler. In aerated water, the hull sinks lower in the water and this wider section then adds stability to the kayak; an incidental advantage of a design feature dictated by competition specifications.

White-water racing demands a combination of the paddling technique of a sprint paddler, and the skill of handling a kayak on, and choosing the fastest route down a white-water river. The competition is a race against time, each competitor being started individually and timed over the race course.

Surf kayaks and skis

Surf kayaks are high-performance planing craft that handle more like surfboards than ordinary kayaks. They are short, and have a flat hull which provides great manoeuvrability when planing on a wave. The seat is near the stern in order to prevent nosediving when running straight down a wave. Good surf-riding demands a high level of paddling skill and a good rolling ability, so the surf ski, basically a surfboard with a seat and footrest, became a popular alternative. A less experienced paddler when upset can simply clamber back on again, cutting out the need for a long swim to shore in order to empty out. For the more experienced paddler, a lap strap and ankle straps enable the ski to be rolled. Surf skis, or wave skis as they are often called to distinguish them from the surf life-saving skis, are mass-produced in rotomoulded plastic, or are custom-built from shaped blocks of rigid foam, coated in GRP. Skis allow more radical shifts of body weight than surf kayaks, but are more demanding on the stomach muscles as the legs cannot help the paddler to sit upright. Skis also require warmer clothing.

Below _Surf skis. Note the foot loops and lap strap._

Paddles

Once you have a good paddle, you will be reluctant to use another. However, paddles come in a bewildering variety of materials, shapes, sizes and prices. So what makes a good paddle? Is one type of paddle the best for everybody, or is it a case of 'horses for courses'?

The shaft

When you pick up a paddle, the first thing you feel is the shaft. Is the hand grip comfortable? It should be oval in section or shaped for your control hand so that you know without looking when you are holding your paddle correctly. Shafts do vary in diameter, so try a few to find the most comfortable.

Paddle shafts are made from metal tubing, GRP tubing or wood. Metal tubing is the most common, and is normally coated in a heat-shrunk plastic sheath for comfort. The shaping for the control hand is achieved by bending the metal into an oval. The cheapest paddles and some of the most expensive have metal shafts. The difference is usually to be found in the quality of the metal used. The higher quality metal shafts have a greater degree of flexibility or 'spring', which makes the paddle more pleasant to use. There may also be a difference in the toughness of the outer sheathing. Metal shafts are not ideal for cold weather, because the metal conducts the heat away from your hands, but most white-water paddles have metal shafts for strength.

GRP shafts are much warmer to handle and are lightweight. They also have a good spring to them. GRP shafts can be made even lighter and more rigid by the use of carbon fibre. GRP is used for racing and sea touring paddle shafts, where lightness is important, although they are also very strong.

Wood is still one of the best materials for paddle shafts. Skilful splicing of different types of wood gives just the right amount of spring, strength and lightness. Wood has a unique feel, and is delightfully warm to the hands. It can be shaped to the required diameter and to an oval shape for your hands. Wood needs to be kept well varnished. I treat this as a winter job, although a touch of varnish here or there may be applied during the season as required. Wood is used for general purpose, touring and racing paddles. For extra light weight, racing shafts are often hollowed. In 1989 the 'double torque' paddle shaft was introduced, with kinks in four places to increase leverage and give a more comfortable hand angle. These shafts are suitable for most branches of kayaking.

Paddle blades

Firstly, should you choose flat, curved, spooned or wing blades? Flat blades used to be very common, as the cheapest blades were constructed from flat plywood. However, now curved blades (which are more efficient than flat ones) can be cheaply produced in plastic, flat blades have become almost obsolete, except for white-water 'hot-dogging' competitions, where the paddles are often twirled above the head or thrown into the air while the competitor rides a wave. Flat blades have no particular drive face, so they can be used whichever way they are caught.

The most common blades are curved from end to end. The degree of curvature varies, as does the width and length. The combination should grip the water well. Small, narrow blades will slip in the water more and lose power when you accelerate.

Spooned blades are not only curved from end to end, but also from side to side. A high degree of spooning makes a blade difficult to control, but it does grip the water well. This design is mainly used for racing; these blades may also have a ridge down the centre of the blade to prevent 'flutter'.

Wing blades work on a completely different principle. They are shaped like an aircraft wing, so that if guided out from the side of the kayak, they move towards the front. Your forward paddling stroke needs to be modified to take advantage of this, starting close to the kayak near the bow and moving out from the kayak throughout the stroke. This type of blade improves performance in sprint paddling, and is also used for fast placid-water touring, but as the blade is of a poor shape for other strokes, it use is limited.

Next, should you choose symmetrical or asymmetrical blades? Symmetrical blades are

Paddles. From top: symmetrical bladed curved paddle, used for slalom, white-water touring and general purpose paddling. Symmetrical blades with cranked shaft (note the blades are set at about 65°), for general purpose and white-water paddling. Asymmetrical blades, for sea touring, inland touring, racing and surf ski riding. Wing paddle, for racing and fast touring.

best for making bow rudder turns, so this design is particularly well suited to the white-water touring kayak, the slalom and the squirt boat. The asymmetrical blade does not perform so well in the bow rudder position, but is better for forward paddling, and is used widely for sea touring, racing and placid-water cruising. It is also frequently used for surfing, where again, bow rudder turns are seldom used.

There is also a choice of materials. The cheapest blades are moulded in ABS plastic; because this plastic will bend easily, blades tend to be narrow, and ribbed lengthwise for strength. Even so, there is a tendency for blades to bend open during powerful paddling, losing efficiency, so although they are adequate and cheap, they are not as good as more expensive blades. Plastic blades are normally fitted to metal shafts.

GRP moulded over a wooden spine makes a good blade. The thickness of the blade determines how strong, rigid and heavy the blade is to be, although thin blades are surprisingly strong. These blades are suitable for racing and sea touring, but for white-water use a metal or plastic tip is needed to protect the end of the blade against rocks. Specialist white-water blades with an internal metal rim are also available.

Wood is a strong and fairly lightweight material for paddle blades, and is used for general purpose and touring blades.

What length of paddle should you choose? Generally, shorter paddles are best for rapid manoeuvring, whereas longer paddles are used for racing and touring. The aim is to achieve a comfortable stroke rate, so a fast kayak needs a longer paddle, while a slow or heavy kayak, being harder to pull through the water, needs a shorter paddle. When I paddle my sea kayak empty, I use a paddle several centimetres longer than when I paddle it fully laden. For white-water touring, surfing, slalom and squirt boating, lengths of 200-210 cm (79-83 in) would be suitable; for placid water or sea touring and for racing, paddles of 210-220 cm (83-86 in) are more common. As a rough guide for a general purpose paddle, stand and hook your fingers over the top of the paddle. The top of the blade should be about level with the top of your palm.

Finally, don't forget that your paddle will need to be angled to suit your control hand. Few

paddlers use unfeathered paddles nowadays, so your paddle will need to be either left-hand or right-hand control. I learned the hard way! All my early paddling was done with flat blades, so when I was offered the chance to buy a second-hand curved paddle I jumped at the opportunity. It was days later when I proudly went afloat with my beautiful new paddle, and discovered to my horror that one of my blades was back to front! I had been paddling for a couple of years controlling with my left hand, and had unwittingly bought a right-hand control paddle! Surprisingly, it did not take very long to adapt to controlling with my other hand, and I have controlled with my right hand ever since. Paddle blades are normally set at an angle of between 80 and 90 degrees to one another. There is evidence to suggest that an angle of less than 90 degrees is less demanding on the wrists, cutting down the chance of tendon problems.

Kayak camping

There is a magical satisfaction to be gained by travelling by kayak with all the necessary camping equipment and food aboard to enable you to camp out overnight. It is an experience I thoroughly recommend.

Loading your kayak needs a little care. The heaviest items should be positioned close behind the seat, with lighter items closer to the bow and stern. All your gear should be fastened in, and your kayak should float on an even keel when you have finished; that is, it should not be bow or stern heavy, and it should not float lower on one side than the other. The cockpit region from the seat to the footrest should be kept clear of luggage so that there is no hindrance to you getting in and out, and items that you may need during the day (such as your lunch and the first aid kit) should be kept accessible.

When you do camp, try to

minimize your impact on the area. Carry all your litter home with you, do not damage vegetation with fires or hot pans, and replace any rocks or boulders you may have moved in order to pitch your tent.

Wildlife

Although in the early stages of your kayaking, you may find most of your concentration taken up by controlling your kayak, as you become more proficient you will become aware that the environment you enter is a living one. Keep your eyes open and you will see a surprising variety of wildlife, both in and on the water and on the shore.

In spring and summer, reed beds and overgrown banks become havens for many nesting birds and wild animals. Please avoid disturbing these areas, especially at these sensitive times of year. A bird book and a wild flower book will add an interesting facet to your paddling, and you will find that the more species of plant and bird you can recognize and identify, the more you will notice.

Equipment for a day trip. 1 exposure bag, 2 waist bag, 3 waterproof stuff sack, 4 waterproof storage bottle, 5 vacuum flask, 6 repair kit, 7 first-aid kit, 8 food, 9 spare clothing with towel and waterproofs, 10 tow line, 11 sun hat, 12 map, 13 head torch, 14 woollen hat, 15 spare paddles, 16 whistle.

Equipment for a day trip

A prudent paddler carries a certain amount of safety or emergency equipment on day trips. This should include a basic first aid kit, a repair kit, some food and a hot drink, an exposure bag, some dry, warm clothing and a whistle. A tow-line, spare paddles and (depending on the nature of the trip and the time of year) a map and a head-torch can also be invaluable. Most of this gear can be stowed in waterproof bags or bottles in the stern of the kayak, and should be tied in to prevent its loss in event of a capsize. For sea touring, a compass and distress flares are required, and in white water, a throw line is advisable.

First aid

Your first aid kit should be equipped for the most likely complaints, which are blisters or minor cuts, insect bites or stings, and headaches (often caused by dehydration in hot weather). There are some very good, compact first aid kits on the market which are designed with the outdoor enthusiast in mind. Check the contents and make sure you know how to use each item.

If in doubt, consult a first aid book, or better still, attend a first aid course. For all watersports, you should know how to perform emergency resuscitation, how to apply external cardiac compression and how to place an unconscious, breathing patient in the recovery position. A knowledge of the signs and effects of hypothermia, its prevention and its treatment is equally important.

Repair kit

The repair kit you carry should at least contain some waterproof repair tape. Plumber's tape will stick even to a wet surface, so it is particularly good for repairing a damaged kayak. Ordinary waterproof adhesive tape is better for repairing paddles.

Weil's disease

Kayakers are at risk from Weil's disease, which is caused by a bacterium that is spread by rats' urine. Most waterways carry the bacterium, which can cause serious illness or death if untreated, although antibiotic treatment is straightforward and effective. Symptoms resemble flu or a chill, and the patient soon becomes very ill.

Rapid diagnosis is essential, and blood samples should in Britain be sent to the Leptospirosis Reference Unit (telephone 0432-277707) for a positive return within 24 hours. If you develop flu-like symptoms following a kayaking trip, tell your doctor to suspect Weil's disease and ask for treatment to be started. Make sure a blood sample is sent to the special unit, as normal processing is too slow and may lead to treatment being started too late to prevent serious illness.

As precautions against infection, avoid capsizes or rolls in slow-moving or stagnant water, wash or shower after paddling, cover minor cuts and scratches on exposed skin with waterproof plaster, and wear something on your feet to avoid cutting them.